Burns

SusanGevirtz

Pamenar
Press

Published by **Pamenar Press**

First Published **2022**

ISBN: **978-1-915341-05-1**
Susan Gevirtz
Burns

Cover design and book design:
© **Studio "HEH"**-Hamed Jaberha

The cover image uses an image of a
6.8" Fossil Crinoid (Isocrinus) that is an
incredibly rare fossil from the Keasey
Formation, Mist, Oregon. This shows
brachia (feeding Arms) and the calyx
(body). Crinoids, sometimes commonly
referred to as sea lilies, are animals, not
plants. They are echinoderms related
to starfish, sea urchins, and brittle
stars. Many crinoid traits are like other
members of their phylum; such traits
include tube feet, radial symmetry, a
water vascular system, and appendages
in multiples of five (pentameral). They
first appeared in the Ordovician (488
million years ago) and some species are
still alive today.

info@pamenarpress.com

to Barbara Guest
Kathleen Fraser
Stacy Doris

Table of Contents

HYPERBOREA OR BERMUDA TRIANGLES I HAVE KNOWN

HYPERBOREA OR BERMUDA TRIANGLES I HAVE KNOWN

—For Genevieve Quick, Jasmin Lim, Margaret Tedesco

A procession of the damned.By the damned, I mean the excluded.
We shall have a procession of data that Science has excluded.
　　　—*The Book of the Damned*, Charles Fort

In the Field of Anomalistics they reside.

Addressing them as sympathetic readers Nietzsche said: "Let us look
each other in the face. We are Hyperboreans—we know well enough
how remote our place is." He quotes Pindar, "Beyond the North,
beyond the ice, beyond death—our life, our happiness."

　　　　　　　　　　　　　　　—*The Antichrist*

Dear Parasympathetic readers,

I am learning to breathe underwater. Finally.

And to see through ice.

Everything I say is true.

But when I talk down here you may not be able to tell.

Ancient astronauts taught me to speak in the gravityless chamber.
You may think what I say is true, and it will be, but my voice will
sound like hers.

Less is more. Less is what we have.

The aquanauts and extreme divers taught me how to access
"documents of the unperceived" (Jasmin Lim) —to hold my breath
for fifteen minutes in order to harvest coral reefs and rings of Saturn.
I come up panting. I come back ripping off my heavy space suit and
holding out a tray of excluded data for you to choose from like
chocolates.

Let's go. But first a spell for insurance fraud. If it works it will protect
us from the bad luck of the ship *Mary Celeste*.

Why did the crew leave the *Mary Celeste*?

The *Mary Celeste*, with a history of misfortune, was said to be "cursed" even before discovered derelict, tables set for dinner, with no apparent explanation. A classic ghost ship, drifting.

In 1885, the *Mary Celeste* was intentionally wrecked off the coast of Haiti in an attempt to commit insurance fraud.

"Anything we measure doesn't correspond… "So: "documents of the unperceived" —Jasmin Lim

Give me your microwaves, radio waves, sine waves and I will surf them "From the transmitter, to the receiver. Across the ether, out of your speaker" —OMD

Or:

Never the Muse is absent from their ways: lyres clash and flutes cry and everywhere maiden choruses whirling. Neither disease nor bitter old age is mixed in their sacred blood; far from labor and battle they live. Neither by ship nor on foot would you find the marvelous road to the assembly of the Hyperboreans.

—Pindar, Tenth Pythian Ode

But the marvelous road calls to us anyway. Landing gear at-the-
ready. On touchdown the craft is swallowed-up. Carnivorous desert.
This the Super-Sargasso Sea into which all lost things go. A stationary
body of water where the gone rises and rains back down on earth. A
sea that takes prisoners like most seas.

They are training me to collect falling things like cisterns collect
rainwater. Get out your speakers. Sometimes you can hear falling.

Collection includes navigating the dangers of the hunt. The outside
of your body is negative space forcing pressure on the skin which
makes skin able to hold the inside of your body inside. If you stop
collecting the pressure abates and skin will not adhere. So collecting
is their breathing.

If the spell holds we continue our journey — another circling attempt
to land. Tighten the straps. Ride above the phenomena St. Fort
was the first to name: spontaneous fires; levitation; ball lightning;
unidentified flying objects; unexplained disappearances; giant
wheels of light in the oceans; animals found outside their normal
ranges. Reports of out-of-place artifacts (OOP Arts), strange human
appearances and disappearances by alien abduction, strange falls,
strange lights or objects sighted in the skies that might be alien
spacecraft. . . .

So now you have met our patron Saint Fort: collector of "damned" data. Who is not a collector of proofless evidence?

Hagiography tells of his marvel on discovering that seemingly unrelated bits of information were, in fact, related. He went back again and again for more data and took more notes. He kept them on cards and scraps of paper in shoeboxes. He wrote in a cramped shorthand of his own invention.

So goes the liturgy. That was a little distraction for those of you who aren't accustomed to heights and depths. Throw that carabineer into the south gust. Get blown off track but stay on the scent. That's the hunt code. Pull your furs tighter. The spell holds. Lean Pole-ward. Rotate your mirrors.

Charroux first related the Hyperboreans to an ancient astronaut race of "reputedly very large, very white people" who had chosen "the least warm area on the earth because it corresponded more closely to their own climate on the planet from which they originated."

Are the poles so bright that we travel through to the other side of brightness? Again we are blinded to the vast prismatic spectrum that prevails there. Borea and Abaris, feasting on gold, show us how to see in the bright.

First they rub their skin with oil of ice. Then they collect plankton,

mineral crumbs, bird saliva, parachute debris, used acupuncture
needles, essence of map, poisonous mushrooms, wings from
downed planes, celluloid film scrap, parakeet feed, anything with
which to make more Rovers and T2 Landers, and anything that falls
from the sky and can be retrieved from a thousand fathoms below.

St. Fort said, "People with a psychological need to believe in marvels
are no more prejudiced and gullible than people with a psychological
need not to believe in marvels." What does belief look like? How
do you advise the parents of a pyrokinetically gifted child to read
Fort's *Wild Talents* rather than the works of Doctor Benjamin Spock?
For this, and all maladies of explanation they imbibe plankton tea.
Plankton is to wander, drift, drive astray. It is the only life form in the
so far north. They serve this tea under the shadow cast by the one
annual sunset.

Fire on the moon, underwater military bases, number stations,
unmanned nuclear lighthouses, thunderstones, fairies, devil's
footprints, giants, evidence for occult criminology

0000000000000 zero zero zero: the sign-off for number stations

In the stars we are dust but in the dust we are hyperstars visited by
the child who has lost her mother. Our aim is to help her make many
return visits to the sky. So we build ships and document the sun

splash crawl space through which she may climb

    Never the muse is absent

    when maiden choruses whirl

    And dervishes lend their spin

    to this paper airplane

Let us look each other in the face parasympathetics. Let us take their cue and wipe off our faces

Tossed the notes to the north wind

Take it. Fold it. Hold it high. Mutter the sound of Ezekiel's sandals walking across the valley of dry bones. Take his hand. Launch it

Fort: "I believe nothing of my own that I have ever written."

GIVE

GIVE

Finance, like time, devours its own children
—Honoré de Balzac

All things are an equal exchange for fire, and fire for
all things, as goods are for gold and gold for goods
—Heraclitus Frag. 90

Just as the waves

need something to break on

so the shore is fed its fabulous share of shell, bird and slow drink

Who isn't stepping on the rotted

following their scent like my dog

If to counterfeit is death who isn't loving

being killed by making more

a taxidermy of what's what

Just as the waves go back and the landing recedes

exchange accomplished and no one can say

Here it began now ends because no one can

mail speech fast enough into the slot between the sea

and the sea

Just as money changes

hands you'll see the tide

is in debt to shore

shore at threat of thug waves

languish in pleasures of supine submission

two-story high tree on its side

tribute to the queen of sands

open-palmed it only exists

when passed from one to next but you

are not there when I reach that cove

Manacle me to the hope of

retribution as repayment and I will

love the owe you've wrought

Shore sighs as you revoke

Waves pummel hope of transfer

If I did

How would I know

X's reciprocal shine

mirror spark

I wanted to give a present

But just then the missile at the Nike Missile Base rose from the
ground

signaling a time of cancelled gifts

Just as when I was 15 and wanted to bestow on a beloved

But thinking I had nothing

bought a white baby rat and was surprised by his surprise

$ is a surrogate

pregnancy passed from one
womb to another uterus use
or any house for commerce

I wanted to give but it looked like keeping

Silent shore   crenellate recede
low tide concession
give and give back the numbers uncountable
I bought or stole a bar of sun

Strode out
and returned tick-laden
arthritic the day acrostic

I needed an arbiter / I needed a money changer / I needed someone
who could count / I couldn't count but could sweep / could
sweep up the change / and mail it to the kids my age in the photos

Needed a vigor / that could fall / forward and away
I wanted to start

or continue something rolling

Supplier – Client relations already in play – I made young donations

I have to

sleep now

head on sand

please leave

this shore

has no more yield

As if all's well as

sites of exchange exit

only as an idea

afloat out there

exists only in being used

So when the tide is saving

its secrecy makes a profit

private

shell game

covenant

hand

it over

If you want a boundless grammar cambio is your passport
visit the denominations window
We share the empty waiting in the wrong line

Who does not quantify? Who does
not count their fallow assets plow their soil under deeper
Surf the double coincidence of wants — and you will

cast the hand-hold wide

and the fantasy that it's measurable will compost
in my back yard no longer mine
We will eat our waste in separate salad resurrections

tide trades with the shore
And there is no escape from this tirade
Silent trade
those who can't speak one another's languages
talk in
owing and withering
of the state
if cashless
you or a witness or an alleged accomplice can
testify can fortify
that it's measurable

Changes hands, membrane, incision, decision
what washes up tide table
debris on a palm read, shore pummeled

you can't trace

whose hands it has touched
such secret genealogy hides history
murder gets away with

borrowing is lending
in need of a single word for buy is sell

I need to be benighted by the benign — drink it up

Was snowing salt
drifts on the ground
Bees feeding on snow
Snow bees changing weather into honey
from stone to salt to snow to the apple-core shape in which the bees
 appear

I need an infinity sign in neon to believe in

spending is speaking
as if the sea needs salt to stay
awake all night
As if the sea itself can't

If your title is too great, too heavy to carry
exchange it for silver
fish > shell > bead
water > shore > salt > scrim
I'd cry and swim if I thought those cheers
would rouse you

He is counting his
other hand cannot be seen
Numerals and obsessive accounting is
the Morse code of what cannot be unsaid
excess a felt contract of redistribution of
emotional resources — a kind of sublimation
After the end of the world start with precious metals
to cross borders

Say preppers and survivalists:
"if you need food, and I have food, and you tell me you can trade
gold or silver, I'll laugh in your face and tell you to hit the road. I
can't eat, drink, wear or live in your gold."

Hit the road or Saltway
Via Salaria
The Salterns, the salt routes, salt highways
and saltpans
Trade routes, ancient roads and tracks
Who eats salt without meat or tomatoes
finger in the jar

Blue hour, golden hour

If I were to march in ritournelles
and you slept next to me
as if nearby
Would you call it a deal would you dream
as a dealer
not me, mine is awake
in the blue-gold horn

Apparently the waves
grab birds from the sky
and the sky
supplies pace
to the sea
like movie music
a common destiny
not all
partnerships are nation states united by the same
currency

I used to be money now
I'm   first
writing was in sand now
it reads washed up bone or bag

To reduce the possibility of forgery
the behavior and the behaved must merge in
what the
sea has
seen
has said

when you
weren't looking
were sleep speaking

As in the 10th century AD when the ocean receded exposing vast flat
evaporation fields, making salt available in increased quantities. Sea
coast salt making was thriving while the land, divided up and handed
out, made owners

Or you could eat paper money
Just as the
shells turn
into beads
You turn into
distance /disguise
digesting itself

Just because you can't see
the spill the
spill is still there the tar
On your bare foot and in your cup

just because
a lifejacket loses its stuffing
wet and mangled at your feet
doesn't mean the one who wore it is

nearby between one event
and another accidental beach
necessary relations cause
happy accidents aka tragedies

The catch, wave-rider
the bodysurf
too close to rhythm
to latch on
to nurse

All day long little notes
passed worth
and forth
wares minted by wish
to touch by paper

appearance or shadow

unearthing ghosts and counterfeit ghosts

thereby proposing a rhythm

If you are a phantom and I am a

phantom's treasure

we will go hunting for shipwrecks

and call that our venture

If there is a tonal

structure to the tide

it helps us grasp

refrain not rondo

Intimate clemency a kind of coin

immaterial corn kernel ventriloquist

By an act of congress you are worth like a man

tucking in between

the language of wares speaks the tightened belt

while the rabbis consider is

credit or belief the sign on Cain's forehead

A pun is counterfeit grail plentiful table

cornucopia of loaves, fishes, earthly divine nourishment everything

stands in for a truer wanderer the gift the container

is found in what it's in

or words hold you till the shyster boat ticket smuggler

says "launch" regardless of night day or weather conditions

no choice the difference between disembodied obedience

gratitude and obligation the word is blank check

but largesse — even if death-sentence-journey — demands counter
    gift not repayable

so the hoarder tries to say something with things

a source
of mercy is not merchantry though the confusion between bread and
    joke is common

his purse is his person

brine left surfeit love when the waves finish up the shore
excess voided contract leaves
a print sometimes erased washes fully away

I woke up thinking
dead thing
what are you worth
tagged or eaten

What do you
want a coin
or a word a seme goes both ways
without translation

You give the ship a direction to follow

And the sea agrees in current and guide

makes debtors of sailors

who burn pyres to its whims

The grace in receiving is all for the giver

I want to give up
longing live without
that crack
unavailable worth
wrath
charm crime
wizard profit

I woke up thinking
sewage
failing infrastructures
and the soon impossibility
of living anywhere without
excess E. coli

If I do not

See what you saw

But I see

you seeing it

now that I

am also

swell you can hear
annunciation
hold your tongue
since can't the tide

Let's not
say we
use the sea
but let it use
us as if choice chooses

its food even uneaten
is us its weather our bloodstream
actually
cover your face
in red cliff clay
turn
into it

Went in
all the way
again, swimming pool otter
underwater sprinter
preferring the heavy quilt
of x-ray bib wave-cover
comfort

Crucible chrysous
First bowls are
gold concave increase
gathers — only to
crash with a set later

even the tender blow

a mistake

Go under tumult

waves or whatever has its way

Turbulence thought above just lay

stomach to sand in the still

spot beneath

as in the bottom

of anesthesia

paid in salt

brine lipped

inverse reciprocal favor

Name the happened disappearance pretense to presence
Intimate amnesty
There was nothing left to leave
Slow fade bewilderment

There was no
redeemable one
disembodied eucharist

thanks in food for food
all the way back to gag
mom holy meal loyal bulimic lender
animal husbandry generation
A usurer of words my brothers are Jews all others are animals
Thank you

Adding is overeating
a kind of buying
for whom do you labor
wanting more of more
makes product viscera
for stocking shelves

Sterile? Generator minus child? Stale?
Portia "The full sum of me"
Only a life can pay
for a life
is slavery
seeks the identically
exchangeable revenge

Emerson says the only real gift is fruit or flower

So hoping for gratitude is spiritual usury

Just like a little unarmed child
draped around her dog

Pay off creditors by believing in them
Truly you both want something opposing
from the same transfusion

Who fulfills herself when dispenses her own good and is thus
immeasurably rich when dispenses her dispensation — poetry or
plowing — these the stadium needs
A play for the court, a movie for the impoverished
distraction from scarcity requires artists just as
Plutus needs paper and signature
Mining is imagining translated into property

Without universal equivalent barter thrives
a mirror as much as money as much as a dictionary

Blinded by care
guarantee the future for something not given
unconditional income

mort gage   dead pledge

a link that separates

bleed for me or at least
sacrifice a lamb
if you want to give a real gift
resuscitate someone in the box you hand me

dare to give do not
forgive the giver
bastard bestower

shameless
love the gift not
our action on each other

daughter bright
as the glistening metal
the King loved so much

Cancellation and redemption
Reckoning or calculation
The infinitesimal smallness of the naught

You may not mint
If you want to make coins
go ahead but it won't even buy you
milk private citizen

A statement cannot become a thing
it is already
never legal tender

A coin in your palm presses
anticipation to explanation
for which there is no resolution

The minter with a stamp
the writer with the inverted world
graven images
it always comes back to
icon and iconoclast
image server gift giver
takes us to dinner without us
a joint stock company, family, purchase, sale
the eater of the plot
not present at this board meeting
votes as if salt exists
for tongues in safety deposit

You say "we can help
each other" and I say what if
help is debt amnesty
behold the Walk Ons
keeping track
quantifying favors
love isn't Jubilee time
for long
always bonded by mutual

dross the false
embroidery
fools gold
the unreal is truer but all
worry aims to free you of
worry

The spectrum in your face
closer to sleep than waking life
participant only in the counting house
behold the beloved beheld
life raft jammed with denizens
perforations where people were
the sea stateless where beholden
the spectrum between sleep and
waking taken

The hen contains the 2nd term
in the first nest
Cling
to temporary status
better than none
helping does not

make a narcissist
less or alien more

Divide feeling by quantity to produce exactness
and love of numeral will reign
The unfathomable
concrete as want
shared by every wisher

Ponzi the sea so "please" makes
an order not an order
but to be as untraceable as bitcoin
we would have to
graft currencies swallow
and hunger will invade you
throw in a fountain
your wish will disappear
Have it or hack it until
epigenetics reverses the love
of number

rumor of figure as portal

to worlds where

inverse earners gain access

to non-standard time in sinew of wolf and eagle

so the secure static number opens the bottom of the sea

submerge sub-prime thousands of fathoms deep

Rise up

remade worlds of roots, weeds rope

above ground count

like our years

ceaselessly promise endlessly

defer

our living wage

wide open

would be

our mouths

small fish would enter

we would be taxis

birds and barnacles

rolling over

food chain
catching
and dropping off on the way
through the plastic badlands and Farallon islands

In the first nest
the hen lays the golden egg
But by the time the 2nd term is translated
The gold is autumn and passes
like season

Abbots of Unreason and Lords of Misrule
Mock king of the New Year's feast of fools
rob spank drink clown
wreck's rouge hours
at the comber of beach sands

wielding the detector
waking lost larder
hunting for metal

Motion Picture Home

Program Notes

Finally but most importantly, the material aspects of its equipment and the intellectual aspects of its performances are in the closest possible connection with the interests of the listener. What kind of power can the theatre generate by comparison [to radio]? The use of a living medium and nothing else. Perhaps the situation of the theatre has been led into a crisis in which no question is as important as the following one: What can be said about the use of the living person in theatre?

—Walter Benjamin, "Theatre and Radio: Toward
the Mutual Control of Their Work of Instruction"

Motion Picture Home is a play that interrogates what a play is — what a play enacts — does or can do —even what the dimensional world can do — even worlds that seem not to be dimensional.

It performs a refusal, rehearsal, inability to perform — where does performance take place? Where is the stage and what can an audience expect to witness there? What is the use of the living person on stage? — Of living in theatre? If almost nothing "happens" on the stage, where might that nothing propose that living, happening does occur? What is *happening*?

If the performers and audience are as much "listeners" as seers, then the spectacle of an audience, being confronted with, included in, the problems of a play, an interrogation of its conditions, as the substance of the play — in addition to an ongoing dialogue of interrogation — becomes the noise of mind, of minds at work, as the action of the play, a play. — Is this what happening is?

MPH engages death, decision, perseveration, conflict, the face of possibility, thwarted possibility, the tension between speech and speaking, and the question of the bridgeable or unbridgeable gap between speech and action, speech as action — the question of what intention has to do with executed action, if anything, and the proposition that motion is equivalent to being alive — and so asks: what then does *alive* look and sound like on what stage? Do plays enact the alive? Is poetry as play, at play, the way life recognizes, runs into itself, on this or that scene of intention? What is a play that demonstrates, mimics, performs, motion? Does that play require human bodies? Is this a play whose script is radio?

What does language without executed action — without correspondence in the three — dimensional world — not as one to one reference, but as action in itself- look and sound like? The language that is not about life, but is, itself, life, alive — is in a sense not in need of a stage, is simultaneously stage's place and action. Then the three-dimensional becomes a redundancy — but redundant in a most fascinating sense: that words and thought be simultaneously translated in object and gesture — that the boundaries between word, object and gesture break and duplicate — be witnessed in the act of breaking down and repeating. That the words of object and gesture make a fabulous show of redundancy, a cacophonous cocoon of thought-life, multiplied to the infinite power.

In 1988 my Grandfather died in The Motion Picture Home, now renamed the Motion Picture & Television Fund. He was a conductor and music supervisor at Universal Studios for 25 years. Among many other works, he scored and conducted the music for *The Benny Goodman Story* and *The Glenn Miller Story*. Short bursts of the soundtracks from these are in the play. Many stars have spent their last years at The Motion Picture Home, as have less famous people from behind the scenes of the industry. It is located in Woodland Hills, Los Angeles, California, on Mulholland Drive.

In the play:

—Voice-over 1, 2, 3 and 4 [*some voice-overs are live but delivered from off stage, some are recorded; live Voice-over 1 is the same person as recorded Voice-over 1, etc.*]

—Teleprompter: as both machine with screen and live voice character

—Time Lord, Sir Sanford Flemming, inventor of standardized time, English accent

—Woman

— The Little Dog

Underlined sections indicate recorded voices.

Otherwise the play is spoken live off stage, with the exception of the "Woman" character who occasionally speaks when on stage.

The script is read at a fast clip

[*Dark on stage. Teleprompter lights up and continuously scrolls these words on its monitor screen:*]

Teleprompter:

And all the motion came home and
all the moving parts came to rest

Stage lights come up and the set can be seen: a big TV monitor sits near the back and a slide of a big touch-tone phone (keypad has large digits for sight impaired) is projected on back wall. Sound of TV static— channel gone off air. Teleprompter to side of stage.

Voice-over 1
(*with static still on*): Was that the final time?

Voice-over 2:
No, rest keeps refusing to be final; keeps being interrupted

V1: I want to see rest. Can you make it visible?

V2: As visible as

V1: You're too hungry for action.

V2:

It's like an anorexia for motion

V1:

Get dressed

V2:

Orders?

V1:

All dialogue is assignments.

V2: So you expect me to respond? [*Pause*]
Listen. I know how to shut you up

V1:

Tell me everything

V2:

You might think I am; you will expect to see something, as usual. You will think I'm giving you something to see

V1: Now get ready for bed!

Teleprompter: [*slightly mocking and sing-song tone*]
Come on get dressed, get ready for bed, put on your rain boots. Not orders — schedules, itineraries — this is how the train runs, this is how the water boils

This is how I, the Teleprompter, tell and tell and tell and tell

[*Pause, TV static stops, then teleprompter voice continues in a different neutral narrating tone*]

She lives in a house near the sea. She goes into it. The air is warm. One man lives there but is never

[*V1 and V2 start to read from the beginning of the play again here. They read on top of the following narration. Each time either the "Woman" character or Voice-over 3 speak, a line from the first part of the play is read over or almost over the succeeding "story" narration. The volume of V1 and V2 varies. Sometimes all of the story narration is run over in this way; sometimes the timing is different and only parts of it are. STOP will indicate when this interrupted narrating ends*]

....home. Three women are in the house when she comes back.

Woman: [*walks on to stage, carrying a pile of too many things in her arms: rubber gloves, glass figurines, long florescent light bulb tubes, Morton salt, masking tape, bicycle pedals, tools, machine parts— looking at the slide on back wall of stage she says:*]
I am not happy at their presence
[*She begins to make a pile of rubble out of the things that were in her arms. Begins to work with salt, pouring it on the floor...*]

Voice-over 3:

She searches the house with her eyes to see what could be violated by them. A partially open drawer full of shreds of curled purple paper presents the first possibility. She says to herself

Woman:

It's purple cabbage

V3:

Do you remember what to do with it?

Woman: Take a fistful and put it on a table. Take out the musical score paper.

[Woman speaking this as she does it, referring to herself as "she."] She takes one strand at a time and places it carefully on the bars. Then when the strands are arranged they merge with the paper and become music, which she can hear or they turn into flat words on the bars of the paper.

I look back at the three women. They are squabbling with each other

V1:

Each starts reprimanding and yelling. She yells back

Woman:

Get out! Get out!

V2: They begin to cower and leave

Woman:

I follow them out into the dirt street and keep yelling, "Go away!"

[*STOP interrupted narrating ends*]

[*Pause, as if watching the distance*]
They begin to diminish, their postures curve, they age before my eyes, they turn their backs and hurry down the street

[*Muttering as she leaves the stage:*]
Fates? Muses? Musketeers? Mutations?

Teleprompter:
Stop interrupting! I mean interpreting!

V3:
Or what about the one called "House Full of Crickets"?
Or "The Grandmother on a stage?" No,

V1:
Preappearance   it goes from name to name

Who does the dream target? Who forget?
Seal your account book and leave it on the ground

something must have before
the year mill

this is only and merely

grinding called passing

But still I miss remembering

a series of familiar but unknown   that are my

The field comes up to meet a plate of lake

rises

the mirror

face on hinges

Flashlight life

V2:

I now want actors to act, make a gesture of speech that divides air!
Now photograph my mouth up close, like dental work, now turn it
into sound!

[*Same voice shifting to a lower, quieter more gentle and seductive
tone:*]

I want to go right through our autism to become an actual object.
Then our Eastern European ancestors will wake up from their cult-
of-the-child sleep. Finally to touch each other. We could have siesta
sleeping together one afternoon over the phone.

[*Normal more neutral tone again:*]

The characters all want me to work for them. I am their whore, but even though they pay me I have to seduce them to let me work. Then they make sudden appearances and disappearances at whim, like a father waving good-by before going out for a death bike ride — all so casual that the mundane and the extraordinary shake hands canceling each other out. Let them work for themselves for once!

[*While the Teleprompter talks the woman goes on to the stage and turns the TV on. Sound of static starts up again. She exits stage*]

Teleprompter:
You have a name but that is not enough to be a character
How could you fall asleep when you were supposed to be building the diorama
I mean watching the kids

[*Pause*] In brackets, as if written by the other author who is reading: "I am second-sight impaired, thought the author" — Cixous.

Scorched garden. Burnt offering. The beginning. No. Burnt garden. Scorched sun. Offering no beginning. Digging here in the ashes the only starting, starling, startling. What I have left of you: a stone from the path where you fell. Perfect for your chest. But your burial was not yours, or ours — burial of complicity, someone else's wish disguised as second guess

V3: [*coyly, like telling a secret about stealing:*]

Confiscation. I am confiscation

V1:

Break and enter   broken and entered

The dark of broad daylight. You all want to steal it for your story

V2:

And then once arrived. The once I'd been planning on plotting for so long

[*Woman enters stage pushing a surgical lamp on wheels and stops it above the rubble, positioning the beam so that it shines directly on the rubble. Then she stands to the side and speaks and gazes as if she is watching what she narrates as it is re-enacted on the stage in front of her. TV static noise comes up again, first very loud, then more quietly as she speaks. A few words into her lines a band saw starts up and continues intermittently throughout this "story". The band saw noise stops when the word* **"STOP"** *appears in the script.*]

Woman:

He who is dead knows he will be dying in a few hours

I ask his guardian to bring him to me

a smallish apartment dark and shadowy

They come in the front door. He walks unsteadily and with assistance only. He comes towards her and takes her face in his hands smiling broadly — no words are exchanged. At first

A light turned up and permeating from his body empties into the
room

He holds her face and utters words words blessing-like
incomprehensible

The guardian guides him to the couch where he lies down and dies.
The car he arrived in is a station wagon and he is now taken out to it
on a stretcher and put in back

"He will be taken to a mortuary," says the guardian.

The guardian returns some hours later with his body. He explains
that the mortician refuses to touch the body because the dead one is

Teleprompter:
From the old country

Woman:
And so his body wrapped in a white shroud, is brought back into my
house and

"what will I do with it?"

[*Phone slide is hit with light; TV static gets louder*

*Woman lies down trying to cover herself under the rubble, then uses
a towel like it's a blanket. Closes her eyes.*]

Voice-over 4:

I remember that

V3:

But I never told it to you

V2:

Did I ever tell you about your Great Great Uncle? He was a highly respected Doctor in Lithuania and one of his patients was a man of the cloth. The man made a lot of money, but, as a religious man, wasn't supposed to have it. So he gave it to your Great Uncle, the Doctor, to keep for him. Then the priest died and there your Great Uncle was, left with all of this money. [*STOP band saw noise*] And a gigantic secret. The shock of this news of the Priest's death made your Great Uncle lose his ability to speak forever.

[*TV static softer in the background now*]

V4:

Here comes the little dog again

The Little Dog:

This is a song called "Vice Grip"
[*Sings*]

Beat you into tenderness

The high art of carrot peeling

The invincible shield

of caring

a weapon from the sky

Against being dead

Voice-overs 1 and 2 [*almost in unison, more like stuttering:*]
The mask? The... The.... The....

The play keeps taking place on another stage. We've tried binoculars, smoke and mirrors, semaphore, etcetera

[*Woman gets up, breaks some of the long light bulb tubes and continues breaking, glass figurines, and other things through the first few the first 20 or so seconds of the sound of the radio, which comes on next after Voice-over 4. Then woman exits stage*]

Voice-over 4:

The first night she slept sitting up

at the feet of the granddaughter on the couch

[*Sound of radio quickly changing channels begins now and continues through "Story" ends when it says **"STOP"** in the script*]

"I have to admit I was scared to sleep alone"

 On the radio psychics and psychic experiences

"Don't take a shower, it's too cold... No you can't. That would be stupid... No... Not now

[*barked out as a series of urgent orders delivered with an edge of disdain*]

Your hair is wet   Wrap it in a towel   Turn the heat on Ohhh, no heat   Dry it very well, don't let it hang on your neck We should eat soon   Why don't you make the   That's not how you

That's the only way   otherwise you ruin   Don't you realize?!

Teleprompter:

I was your eyes

but no longer

do I lend you sight

meaning, you arrange your own exile dealer

[*TV static off*]

Voice-overs 2 & 3 in unison:

We'll give you a play by play of what can be seen from here

[*radio stops*]

Voice-over 3:

Due to the problems of duration and space, nobody can actually watch it. The Los Angeles earthquake has just occurred. The story is recalcitrant. Lassos slip off. It becomes exhaustion as artifice as performance to even try to begin here.

The little dog:
[barks a few times before beginning]
Little song, little song, we need some rain or something to get us out of this. Give me a treat!
[Dog sings:]
Who are all these extras, stunt men, make-up and hair people? Endless supply of population. This is distraction. Let's return. You're too famous for this

*[Dial tone. Sound of dialing (old fashion non-digital) a phone number and dial tone continues over script until says **"STOP"**]*

V1:
Incidentally, a few years ago, when it was still a bright color, I cut off a hunk of my hair and put it in tissue paper in a drawer in the bathroom. Next time you're here I'll give it to you and you can put it next to a picture of me.

[Dialing and dial tone sound continue but more quietly]

Teleprompter:
Okay, Let's start over

V1:

Call me a new name this time

[***STOP*** *dial tone and dialing sounds*]

Time Lord:

I am the Time Lord. I see you are waking up. Will there be enough
time in the day for you today?

V1:

All I need is...

V2:

He said start over

V1:

Okay okay dengue virus, reinfection, iteration and reiteration of
impossibility, iteration times X

V2:

Times ekphrasis?

V1:

Don't try to be clever. By time I meant a long 90 minutes
But that was not it the luxury
the plenty either without
imagination to offer anything
else...... But that was not it

either thought

to offer etc.

words

last

the last speech was in words

V2:

And you confused time, words, Canadian and Scottish currency?

V1:

Someone did. Look up the word currency

V2:

You're hoping to introduce a problem aren't you?

V1:

Shhhh... Give me your hand, I'll take you down by the sea again

V2:

It's too late for that lullaby

[*Pause, quiet*]

Everything is for the first time   again

Why I am here: Can't see straight

Can't see what seeing looks like

Sleep eludes me   taunts from across the river

Desire dead in the ditch at the side of the road

V1:

Can't it be resuscitated?

V2:

I'm going to ignore you

As I was saying, learning the world one by one

You suggest
  hide in the forest of a car
I can't do that
You suggest
  wear the dead man's clothes
can't do that
You suggest grow childhood up in one year
Not that either
Nowhere to find the seam

V1:

Change all the locks on the doors?

V2:

Maybe

V1:

Can you go away and forget?

V2: [*long pause*]

Colophon

elegiac sands

the gated mouth
subdivision tension
Mouth and Magician

    Lifted from the margin
where he no longer is
      There is a room   There's room   Now
he's more More everywhere   — the visible and the
invisible are too small   The container needs a
new name: not body, not assembly, not variety

Teleprompter:
SCHISMATIC SCHISMATICS at best
[*Slide changes from phone pad to the word SCHISMATIC as
Teleprompter speaks.*]

Time Lord:
What you need is a glass bottom boat and a ring that allows you to
talk with animals. If the word and day don't match, tear the hair out
of the day. I can see eight Barbies sitting around an oval dining room
table. They are all dressed up for dinner and ready to be served. A
woman comes and begins pulling their hair. One by one each is given
some nasty yanks instead of dinner. So, find a new word if it doesn't
match. An unfinished puzzle is a dinner disaster.

Woman: [*from off stage:*]

If this is someone's storage, I mean story, why are they never
allowed to speak?

[*Pause, silence, no answer, she continues*]

waiting? forgot the combination? cancer of the vocal chords...?
All of the above....?

Teleprompter:

Do you have to rush us? Stories require less pressure and plays
require a tourniquet. We've sent for one. Delivery is slow these days.

Time Lord:

Which raises the question: Can you die twice? Can you plan it that
way?

V1:

The prophecy usually comes in the beginning but I can see it on the
horizon now

V2:

Nervous system as geiger counter goes haywire. On coming home.
Picklocks. Contagion as love. What does "willing to go toward" look
like after amputation, sedation?

What has happened? The severe blow to the head of a dried-up river
named Disappointment, named Contingency

So reread the prophecy from this rickety shack:

Not contingent but related

Standing in the gulf between the done and the done

Tertiary

V1:
D is for Dare

V2:
Or D is for gas lit. Love's gas lighting.... fill in the blank   His face,
how will I go on seeing it?

V1:
Did the prophecy say: D is for Unauthorized?
To not act or say
to suspend
active suspension
"The ocean does not try to make low tide"

[*Teleprompter screen stops scrolling the words:*
And all the motion came home and
all the moving parts came to rest
and starts scrolling the script of the play from the beginning]

Time Lord:
My turn! On that forty-four-day passage in 1845, we, the Flemming
brothers nearly died. On one fearful night in the midst of a North

Atlantic gale, I took readings of wind speed and direction, calculated
the ship's heading and tonnage, and determined that we might not
survive until morning. I inscribed this sober assessment, adding a
declaration of faith in God and a profession of filial gratitude, bottled
the note, and threw it overboard. Naturally, my life being one long
monument to industry and good fortune, the bottle was picked
up on a North Devon beach and delivered to my parents not many
months after I'd settled in Peterborough, my first Canadian home. [1]

V2:

I'm tired of you! You enrage me! I miss the little dog. I miss
tantrums!

V1:

Not me, I am in love with you — my intimate assassin, visible
planet, age of steam. I love it when you say,"Time's one visible
analog is space." Say it again — for you time and longitude are
interchangeable: time keeping, bee keeping, "five quick inches of
snow," a missed train, a misprint, whose fault? Talk to me in the dark

Time Lord: [*a little more intimate tone*]
When time is an inherited private property, nothing that reduces its
value can be negotiated. So you might as well love me. You have so
little choice anyway. [2]

V2:

Partition or parturition? that is my question

Voice-over 4: [*softly says:*]

Relax, you don't have to compress it or tell it fast. All the time in the world in a vice grip is over. Remember?

V1:

Of course I don't believe you. It goes like this:

In that low lying flatland
        no explanation
And no explanation can rest or fish without gills
    or lungs without breath
Called to witness and summarize
     eyes cut out of the face place
The low lying delta lands where only drainage
     only refuse, only debris, body parts
from the wrong animals trying to string themselves
     together, blood through unmatching veins

This the La Brea Tar Pits of gesture
only the evidence only remains
distilled to a black viscous wash
immovable   This sea between will and wish
gone awry   we will meet there
never

V2: [*exasperated tone*]

You are a bottom feeder! Can't you do anything else? I need to win a vacation from you.

V3:

I hear a storyteller pulling up to a pier. A [pause], A [pause] and A.

V1:

Never leaving A. No futures

V2:

I wouldn't call this a problem. I'd call it data.

[as if reciting a nursery rhyme, sing-song:]

fruitless   restless

irreconcilable   differently configured

Q is for Quandary

           Quarry

           Query

partakes of one kind of world

     while the other languishes

          perishes is parched

into the coffer

     the stranger

pioneer more

this given distance on obsessiveness

V3:

There are two reasons why I am here. And they are the same reason.
One: always keeping what is most known at a remove — so far at a
remove that I can't recognize myself in my surroundings. Two: my
surroundings, that which provides so...

By "surroundings" what is meant? Anticipation. Of the read and
unread what has not yet been read and unread. It who can take this
into account and return a renewed uncanny.

V1:

It?

V3:

Yes. I was an embryo suspended in liquid nitrogen once, just like you.

V1:

Guilty, heavy, and obsessed with escape?

V3: Yes. Night Reuters reported on me. They called me a "human
body shop." My crime was what I had to offer. Safely suspended in
space I couldn't stop dreaming of Winnicott — the deck of my ship,
the voice who secretly let me out to play alone.

Now I have to rely on binoculars. Here come the large puppet people
and the small mouse people: No sense of proportion and no one
stays the same size

[Woman comes on stage and begins arranging the salt, drawing in it, etc and uses masking tape]

Time Lord:

Don't get too elated. The mismatch doesn't go away. See how hard it is to keep track of us without seeing us? That's what I mean: word and deed, word and day, name and night — we are a beautiful pageant of parthenogenesis

V2:

Yes. Succession of days. As if a day can succeed. But it's almost sad. That's the only way he knows how to tell the story.

V1:

Have no pity. Everyone owes him money!

V2:

Okay. We are finally at the Terminal. Stage right. Stage left. There are other things that return too.

V3:

Yes, double crescent moon
the never seen before in balmy pre-spring darkness
a slight fog haze in front of the moon
so its bottom curve is a double claw
in the sky

V2:

[with a little laugh/tone of disbelief and incredulity]
Are you trying to talk about beauty?

V3:

No, it's just that we all need somewhere to go. I was on the way
to the airport. Trying to infuse it with life it doesn't have and then
backing off to see if it could inflate itself

V2:

I've heard of this, "come from afar thinking." Thinking arrival is
possible

V3:

An anemic caucasian albino

V2:

The pigment taken out of all loophole

Teleprompter:

We had to leave the rank fields. We had to do our plowing
elsewhere. You will never understand this. You on your paved road
under refracted sun.

V1:

The presence of the person who resides in the poem enacts what
the poem can't do, does, through description of daily acts, she and
he commit

V2:

Murder?

[*sound of dial tone*]

V1: [*frantic, as if warning of danger:*]

Get away   Get away   Get away from

Woman: [*looking up from what she's doing with the rubble, but not at the audience, her voice recorded, not her actual present mouth, says calmly, in measured speech, as the band saw starts up again this time in intermittent very short spurts:*]

The routine does not solidify instead it undoes solidity, undoes...
I think this is not what you'd expected....

[*She leaves the stage and says in person, not recorded, from off stage:*]

A few possibilities: Carve a sacred cenote into the chest where rain can collect; put the ice sculpture back in the refrigerator

Teleprompter: [*said as taunt*]
Verge Verge Runaway!

V1:

But I'm talking to you teleprompter: Is hope good for health?

Teleprompter:

Form / to inform / to give form to / to animate / "a moving ratio" [3]

[*Phone slide returns. SCHISMATIC slide remains — they are next to each other*]

V1:

In any case I can't help it, I keep looking forward to the unit, not the person.... In place of the father the guard was in the vestibule writing verses from the bible on a notepad
[***STOP** short spurts of band saw*]

Woman: [*reading script from side of the stage, just barely on stage while recording of following spoken by Teleprompter plays over woman reading:*]

Teleprompter: *simultaneous with the following until it says **STOP** in script. Barked out as orders that repeat:*

Go!   Turn it on!   Dry it!   Eat!   That's not how!   Don't you?!

Woman:

[*Looking down at her lap — tone of grave apology*]

"I'm sorry I don't have more news. Here you are finally and I don't even have anything to talk about

[*Pause, then in a first beseeching tone that turns into yelling:*]

If you're leaving let me up! At least unstrap me so I can stand! Don't go without unstrapping me! Don't leave me like this! [*Pause, then continues more vehemently*]   Let me stand! Before you go unstrap me!

[*Teleprompter **STOPS** barking orders, woman leaves stage*]

Teleprompter:
That meat like the flesh of my own body pounded by what I continue

Teleprompter:
The offspring, the forgetting, then the morning of decision

V1:
Was there relief in the decision?

V3: [*inhales, sighs, says slowly*]
A relief like, like....

V1:
No. Don't search for words. There are two paragraphs that worry me in the book that this play was adapted from. Speaking of the irrevocable! Of things like earthquakes and butchers! One is about the endless desire for response and reflection

V3:
The other is about over-stimulation: "The voice of the master and the one who had to do what the master said.... The desire to get

away from the over-stimulating mother to a secret place where one didn't have to mirror and reflect." But it was a bad translation. I know because it offered this parable:

"from empty goodness to good emptiness"

and named exactly what you want "Zero coercion space" [4]

V2:

And now we're back to where we always started: the mother's body, a moving picture, a constantly shifting configuration

V1:

I can see it now

Time Lord:

Let me know when something happens

V2:

I promise you'll be the last to know

V3:

Skipping a stone on the surface of the future until it sinks is my way of telling time

V1:

Or what the caretaker of a 90 year old said:

I sleep when she sleeps

I eat when she eats

I watch what she watches

Teleprompter:
Eat your heart
heaven

To reveal
to unravel
to show to sew

V3:
I held her hand all night. I slept next to her and it was as if I held her hand ensconced in the ninety-year-old sleep. Asleep in sleep and breathing without diving gear

Teleprompter:
So long you've been dead already and only six weeks. Why do you have to die hundreds of times over so that your death is a portal I can never enter enough

V1:
Even a glass bottom boat wouldn't help with this. No bottom visible through the dense tangle of water plants, leaves and fish asleep in the sun just under the surface. Fish reclining in the sun like cats. The never seen before presenting itself as usual

V2:

The diagnosis: Ventricular Tachycardia —

Or a vasectomy that stopped working. Here, death seems
particularly frail and weak, difficult to maintain, no matter how much
effort I put into the killing

V1:

You like to build with negative space blocks, piling them up till they
almost fall —I want to maintain your punctuation — as an ideal
approximation — as a kind of clock we — not invented but captured
and — not altered but inhabited — it's just that sometimes I forget
you have so much volition

[*The teleprompter screen stops scrolling the play script, returns to
scrolling the two lines it scrolled in the beginning:*

And all the motion came home and
all the moving parts came to rest]

Teleprompter:

Get the suitcase with plane crash all over it fixed
Put in plants that absorb sound

Two hands in surgical gloves

Form's Infirmary
questions unposed   exposed

V2:

Solution is one kind of container

Time Lord:

There is a time when time is up and I'm sorry but it is now

V1:

In what units? Pints of blood transfusion? A hearing test take-home exam?

Teleprompter:

The appropriate question of a container is not, "Is anything in it?" although they beg to be asked....

V1:

Beggars begging from beggars...

V2:

Or something faulty at the site of attachment

V1:

By "site" do you mean Los Angeles?

V2:

Yes all history comes from young Los Angeles

V3:

Where else would they bury someone with her credit cards? If you

can call it "bury" — no soil was involved — more like putting her
away in a marble chest of drawers

V1:

I recall that when this was reported it became an impediment that
no sight-enhancing instrument could overcome — the blocked view
of, was it the future? the past? — that unfolded from this

V2:

Yes, the water cartel, the loss cartel, they thought they could buy
anything then, alive or not...

Time Lord: [*slightly gloating*]

The ancestor of the credit card, the steam locomotive, is my relative

V3: [*Slight aggressive sarcasm*]

Why are you telling us this? Are you proud? — that "Standard time
stands out, stands up as a defining act of social coherence?"...
Whose place are you taking? Segue, tangent — are these your real
names? Handcuff? Strong arm?

Time Lord:

I want meteors in our pockets next to stopwatches

Woman: ....[*comes to edge of stage, barely on, says quietly as if
musing, while writing the following words on the wall in chalk*]
...the children, the inmates, the beekeepers... With whom do you

identify? the crowd? the end?

[*exits stage when finished writing*]

Time Lord:

The children have become the clients... I'm sorry to relay this news
to you. I decreed two kinds of standard time: cosmic and local.
And that the unit measure of time shall be a day absolute... This
information about the children is the result of an exact measurement
taken in an amalgam of cosmic and local time — like an epic, or a
Greek play, it traces the contours of one complete cycle: sunrise to
sunset; nine years of wandering and then return; the prophecy of a
life and its fulfillment from birth to death

V3:

The Annals of Escape? That is yet another story. The Allowances?
Another

Time Lord:

Yes. Not ours. Not the one at hand. I want you to know: humans will
measure what is in front of them. That is my discovery. My psychosis
is that I know there is a most precise way

V3:

And that precision is best?

Time Lord:

Precision leaves out a lot, but I prefer misnomer to error

V3:

Locomotive's motive?

Time Lord:

Well, let me put it this way, are you sad about the children?
Psychosis is a recent invention, as recent as steam, and as imprecise
as

V3:

...as redundancy?

V1:

An emphatic mistake?

Time Lord:

Without measure, therefore immeasurably sad

V1:

Your sadness is my escape hatch — a mistaken emphasis

Time Lord:

I like to make plans and execute them

V1:

What is your favorite method of execution?

Time Lord:

Direct statement

Teleprompter: [*hesitation, quiet*]

But what is there to give that isn't given in time?

[*PAUSE, a little longer than above*

Woman comes out on stage and speaks the following lines in unison with Voice-overs 3, 2, and 1:]

V3:

The house?

V2:

The Home?

V1:

Excised from domesticity does it exist?

[*woman quickly leaves stage*]

Teleprompter:

Welcome Home! Welcome Home! Pictures of the Stars cover the walls and the glory of your life is a glare in your face

V2:

So they wear robes and glamorous sunglasses inside? Their former importance is served at each meal? All in on it together like the builders of the great pyramids: stunt men, conductors, actresses, make-up artists, set strikers, directors, producers.... I could go on

[*short patch of music from The Glenn Miller and Benny Goodman Stories blasts, then turned down continues more softly under the following*]

V1:

The aged of The Industry, all under one roof — Can they still autograph?

V2:

A signature is not a measure — it can't include

Teleprompter:

No fault — What's lost is not the same as what's stolen

V3:

Shhh... the dog is sleeping

V2:

Who is left to be funny?

[*Music stops*]

V1:

Maybe my heroes know: The first weatherman Truman Abbe, the first information operator, the first Delphic oracle...? We could call them up

V3:

Or we have

Time Lord:

Here is my own eerie little time story: When I was a little boy I saw my father put a dime in a parking meter. "How can they be renting time?" I asked. "They're renting space. It just comes out of time", he replied.[5]

V1:

And here is a small inside story... "Nothing is more deceptive than an obvious fact" said Holmes to Watson.[6]

V3:

So parking meters as dowsing rods?

V1: The case? The usual suspects: A ticket to the nearest city, to decision, to a movie house, to action... So what is the case?

V3:

Well, put it this way, she was a different person the moment she stepped aboard. An unwelcome guest...

V2:

Is reception a decision?

V1:

No — more like a discordant — well, full of chords, chemical reaction

V3:

I hear the weather.... which always makes me long for the

weatherman...Not just Truman, but prediction in general, not just a wish, but last words, or first, for that matter...

[*All scrolling stops. Teleprompter screen shows blank until a few pages later when Teleprompter says: "What else can be seen out there?"*]

Teleprompter:
There were years of quarantine, and then... the weekends opened up like chrysali, like sponges in water...

V2:
And we learned the ancient art of sponge diving

V3:
You mean to hold our breath and keep our eyes open for long periods under water?

V1:
Yes, like swimming under radar or time

V2:
Yes, we learned..... we learned that long ago on the Sunday of Two Noons the sundial was banished but the sun could not be

V3:
Matter of time, mother of time....

V2:

It said, "I stay not awake

I go not away"

Nobody heard but someone drew a picture

V2:

It was finally understood that he had nothing else to provide but
provisions

V1:

And autographs were no longer possible with such palsied hands, no
longer rang true anyway...

V1:

Vow of silence   of reference
allows for great turning radius

V2:

Are you preparing to embark?

[*woman walks slowly on to stage*]

V1:

Here the human sees for the blind dog. We are packing, if you can
call it that... actually preparation is a false oasis like the concept of
summer

[*Woman runs her hands over the walls and the slides projected on the walls for about 40 seconds, then leaves stage]*

V3:

Pointing at the picture she says, "That's someone knitting a seashore. They just finished the seaweed part."

Teleprompter:

That's as close as you can get to the sun and that is why some things cannot become facts, death by fire, etc...

Time Lord:

Am I under arrest?

V2:

No just detained and sublimated — we should have gagged you too

Teleprompter:

What else can be seen out there?

[The following words (spoken — not recorded — to end) as they simultaneously appear on the teleprompter screen]

V4:

Plague of example, of pestilence, as if those could serve the purpose of illustration, of conclusion

But it remains unnamed, precludes, eclipses, demonstration, shines on what's not alive making that inert wood recognizable as done, in a way that never otherwise could have been seen

V1:

She points to Spyglass, kaleidoscope, naked eye

Chatterbox Circus, the pages torn out of the old book and placed like tiles all over the floor

V2:

She has learned to say, "My mind is blank."

V3:

...so she can close her eyes and hold one in each hand, considering which is heavier

V1:

She becomes a scale?

V3:

Not a measurer, a conjecture....   unassisted it's just....

....anticipation, before the fact, the only

For my Father, Grandfather, Grandmothers

The Wind in Her
Daughtership's
Majesty: a maske
antemasque

The wind is my mascot
I shall not want

But even the wind
is owned by names

And struggles against its hand

        wind   wind

       the wind so high

   rain keeps travelling

    in the sky

so fine so pretty

She's the girl from the golden city

Los Angeles, Heliopolis, gold rush San Francisco

Willa Clio Emma Zara Sara

in a line in a row in a clutch

Gonca, Siarita, Helen, Angeliki, Eleni, Evangelia, Tatiani

Athens Istanbul Barcelona

Rosa, Carolina, Charlotte, Selene, Lucinda, Vasiliki

line them up mix them up

wind   the wind

snow comes scattering

from the sky

in mourning or just likes black
on the prowl or just likes cleavage

making it up as they go along
picking through the debris to make temporary deals

How can they know they daunt
in their bright efficiency
raise fear in those fumbling to get closer

Do I or don't will won't
rolling the dice and
watching the watchers as they promenade

Sonja Olivia Petra Caitlina
struggling against the hand of their wind

What's in a girl sugar eyes
yes she could might or would

With my heavy watch on I
take my Father's pulse

turn to deflect
the protagonist's punch

I. *The Ex-Remunerations*
    —after Evan Kennedy

exalted in sick diversion from
rather escape hate so many lanes
it offers to the riders I like

the flagged spinning his
bike spokes past the city haunts
thirty and more years the overlay of memory façade

who cares the time doth so ripen rot
on two or four wheels cruise the was will
cashew-held feeding from the feedbag

as when I spun and sped through Los Angeles Wilshire
Sunset boulevards helmetless and dauntless
because only one known person had so far died

and he off at a golf course
having a buffet lunch forever
tasteless not only to my young ears but

also to the palms whose salute eternal
kept them putting what a green of no
return what a grandfather and greater

gave the possibility of talk over breakfast
interest in one another man and girl when
he was gone I saw him everywhere

from my bike, salvation in a city
where buses kept you waiting for hours

You there in the sun so far away from your own home town
Hey what were you thinking not using sunscreen or nursing
and inhaling Kool menthols Put on your tabbies, the sand is
hot. Smear of coral lipstick gash on the grandmother's mouth
dissociated entirely from her words and being a dawning
understanding that in the Grandmother and others there were
at least two: the one present to an audience and the one who
forgot about them And there were some who never forgot,
reapplying theirs immediately after a burger and even on the
way to bed And some even fewer who never thought of them
even when they were there This all began to move out of the
landscape creating a fore and background of the kinds and
with whom affinity could form Seeing that there was too much
attention to the lips yet a fascination with that sport and those
who excelled at it exponentially drawing the audience and
sometimes us to them

up to whose judgement was it uncle of disgust

arbiter of armpit hair

My underwear is mosquito proof as I've sprayed it with the
Korres of the land Here sunscreen abides and the bougainvillea
sea warm wind sun damage also saves the days Overpopulated
heritages not to mention over given not to mention well-re-
ceived not to say that the kids on sting rays going by below are
thinking 'this is my childhood, better make it through, better
drink it up' always aspiring to be the next age when the next is

not really next but a long road of digestion

For you girls to be perked

For the nice to be nursed

For you gals to be paid and to choose who you lay

When the roll was called mine was unpronounceable and
certainly without correction from my court A discipline of
the vigilant whose mind already preferred the window to the
chalkboard Always on an errand to the sensation of the day
wind in face muscle in rhyme back up before back into first
light shallows tracks slip and stay a prowess of element tra-
verse I recall hands off the handlebars too He will understand
how it also was my vocation

all I ever wanted was skill
through sun momentum

when I was that hurry

downhill

II. *First Lie*

A door will open in the air

Undisturbed by experience

Pollen into honey
Honey into captivity
Remedy

First Love

The banal replacement one of another

If the first stands the flailings of the

next may be survived

First Launch

Spoon fed itinerary from a very young age

that the pearl is their oyster should be no surprise
Are all their resemblances effaced in the heat of embrace

Or the train stations of the cross

trinkets in their fists cannot escape

the kinship whose trace draws them along their course

Where sleeveless trials present as decision

They know that beds do not make them local

O kilo and kilometer conversion be a festival of final exam

First Sight

already in the missing beat

voluntary vertigo

the lead-off leg and the couple

first hesitation second dissonance disappearance

Behind suspense

summer backs

potion poured

lips on the glass on the watch the friend

slack spines not theirs

Then trade vigilances and lord it over

Now it's their turn to rush

to the rape and reward fields

sharpened they lean into the keel

discipline their sail

A little secret something or someone polishes

the day while the harness is a chosen diadem

By their shoe choices you will know them

What is that rustling the trees?
Who is there?
What is that blowing my hair?
What makes the sea move?
Who are you?
What goes forever more?
The wind,
The wind will blow
Until the very end
It will rustle the trees
And blow my hair
And move the sea
And blow
Forever more.
The wind.

III. *Error Infirmament*

Gallivant girls palms on

shift revealing momentum in

unfamiliar wish streets

What ritual realizes farmed

out as if fame did it for

the disarmed and their private forms

a vigilant labor

a high maintenance checklist

weary weary a playhouse a puzzle piece

names in full bloom

girlhood's season of no apology while harmed into the saying

the soon to be of it

both hands on the steering wheel Dad

please don't kill us

blinded by your girlfriend's lap

the snowy cliffside so close

The protagonists smitten by us need

us to see us

Backpedal so time a perfect accident delight

saying yes

a useful fiction becomes

his name

cresting for decades an

anticipation direction

don't say cowards but the wise

bide their time and hold back

I mean their restraint

is not a boxed set of

posture hair color poised for pleasures

sun kissed arm flesh

boat-neck string bikini

IV. *Spill*

I felt sorry for them. A mix of pity and compassion. A fantasy of service. As a teenage girl I befriended old men in the park. I thought they needed cheering up. I thought I had a unique capacity to do that. I believed I could be exempt from danger and sleeze. I believed I had a way through the cracks of the given problem. I learned that I was gifted for old men and older women

    wind wind wind

      The rain comes sparkling down

      This little girl says she'll die

I went to bed. Or wouldn't get up. Stayed under the covers at the foot of the bed. Outside bright sun cheer and oaks bore down through the big windows. I turned my back. Curled toward the wall. Something had to be done to show what had happened and it chose me as its signage

What had happened was unclear. I tried to be helpful. When she was gone I carefully unwrapped the things in one of the moving boxes. Tenderly placed the soft bloody swaths in her sock drawer where they probably belonged. But received no thanks for this

keep moisture spreading hydration herding

Their childhoods all led breast-ward
An obstruction to seeing the ground and finding things that
    fall at your feet — or so I thought of my breasted future
thus was happy that mine were late in bloom
We flung and ground and rubbed them together and against
    each other's
Some like tongue tips some like sea anemones some like the
    sea urchins carved from their shells right after she dove for
    them for me
These beasts crustacean swells, harbingers of suitors and
    pretime when we swam
on each other

This little girl said, "Give me a pool and I'll cross under water"

That one said, "Give me an ocean and I'll scale it"
Under any wave I'll find the quiet spot, lie still face down
    calmly and let all

of your turbulence pass over unattended

something pushed me hard under water, a rough hand over
my chest wouldn't let me up At camp on a hike the counselor
put his arm over my shoulder and then further down. A coma
of confusions that will never fully lift

But now I have noticed
that you speak to me like audience
You have forgotten my kinship with the off shore
fins and mistaken me for the custodian of time-keeping you
  may
not realize that the watch and the shore are allies
Allied in my fitness

oh the capacity for breath holding

sing its high praises though we know

it can cut both ways

in not questioning the sequence from Barbies
to girl on girl discovered

the verboten

flickers at the edge of sight

moth to florescent night algae

Did I or did I not see the grunion run? Did I or didn't I scare
away the boys the minute I opened my mouth? This the girls of
the many names wonder. Some more than others

On the other hand the girls and women came unasked and
unafraid, of all ages, curly and straight, in all sizes and strides

You need to figure out the best angle. Head shot from above.
Sideways camouflage. A little is too much. A lot not enough

V. *First Fall*

A plan. A pill. A chicken in hand. A dressing room piled with the discarded

The slap down. The slip up-but why?

An eight-year-old has already plotted and executed one run-away at five years old. And plots the next in front of the TV on which Kennedy was just shot interrupting Lucille Ball

     rain comes sparkling down

   This little girl says she'll die

    For want of a lover with a rolling eye

If you were my daughter and your daughter's mother

I'd wrap you in a flame blanket and roll you to an orchard

Where sentries would feed you oranges and you'd never
  have to learn

That as public property pregnancy is not yours

Flaunt it and fuck it and take your hand off it

When it suits you to agree, okay, or crack your whip and

away he'll go

And if she harms you in the name of misguided fairness

Bring the borderline a gift and turn your back on her

Never think of the reason for it, lock up and hunker down

In your own savings of miles

Enfeebled in the outerlands

Outsider outside the province of promise

VI. *Equation*

Placeholders for futures

You will live among us

Third guess turntablist

Keep steering back

We do lose our ways

Some tunes taunt return

Some return us to us

Literally your neighbors

Don't know you

Yet you yearn for recognition

In disguise as a name

but unpronounceable

Have we been here before

almond eyes

You are not in this room

I am in age days else you distance dictates

joy of muscle stretch

handsome, pretty,

She is the Golden City,

has lovers one two three

Iphigenia, Sally, Randi, Dido, Jill

above any fire break

between here

and the blank boundless

bind on flight or only

In his bosom he will clasp her

Clamp her to the habit of him

She is the flower of one two three

Please to tell me who is he

The time has come to stall no longer

What do you think we do but flounder

Looking sideways through the whistle

Pretty pride has had its day

Let the boys say what they will

Come we're going again

to the field where Morgan and Igraine

three times mend the broken breaking

Santa Ana, Meltemi, Sirocco, Bise, Bora,

Feng, Mistral, Buran, Purga, Burga, Chinook, Fohn, Zonda, Samoon, I will

name you all again

Take you from your beds and harbors call you by the love of hammers

Go to sleep on pillows of new, let the rocking move you still

They will teach us wind prediction

Off to on shore morning breezes

From west to low the mountain caper thistles

Rhythm helps us hike the gorge but drop it

at sight of sea

So and so will never come never go

The wind wind shrill and smart

dances with a broom

Circle and pick

a girl for the center

She must choose a name

Sing, sing

What is a ring game

Sing the middle rots the middle swirls

I saw the promise the delight

the adjustment behind your eyes

I saw the arrangement of compromise

I saw you counting four five six how

did they do it before

resound chorus together we turn
behind they pass us
fist over fist

What I want to say is one thing do another

And wish for you yet a third

Is there an outside or only refrain

beaten up echo

disclaimer to excavate

symptom stung

VII. *Placeholders For Futures*

Do we dream of new captions

or underwrite other lyrics

Do we wish for a safe house

excise the lines plane ticket

Please do tell us what to do

Here start over

Tell me what you are sleeping under

Quilt of weight and promise

Come with the bees and talk in a circle

Heathen cast or pretend another

I'd like to give

the ark

but we have labored in the trenches

And wish to save you

so much grovel

You may win a key
to the golden city
And hope when you
arrive the gold is still sun

Keep steering back

We do lose our way

disabused of rest

brings ambush

If something is

broken sing to it

of a hearth or a hunt or a menu unrent

No, there's a lot I

don't know in your idiom

But still to narrow

the width between

the said and the felt

is an isthmus

of belief

the boat moves toward

It's the leaves blowing

not footsteps behind you

It's the dressed up

but still hungry

in the valley valley
so low hang
Your head
over hear   the wind

This wish made of air

That has undergird so much

fed

the stern grasp

Would

launch

scores of vagabond bicyclists

fleeing

fates so

Left the family compound

with a bowl and a spoon

Asking who we do what for

On her I wait
mundane glory

star of our skit

For the long nights awake next
to your sleep
Who's transfused by second amnesia

longing for night company

A girl is singing into the camera

A camera is putting hands in her hair

I saw you toss the kites on high blow
Birds about the sky

Beast of field and tree

Flowers in the summer fires in the fall

I would deteach

these poles from tendons

Enfeebled in the outerlands

light up my

spine to align with that

tree trunk vertebrae

to vertical

While the sky

calls roll

The wind or a car coming

A car coming or water rushing

So Flora, bride of the west wind

Is it really you who controls all flowers

beyond doer and done

outside the dyad is not

give over not in

Like the new moon the old

forecast in her arms

weather of soup, plans

cell tower censure

Badge winds
Aeolus
Antiklea
Antiope
Phaidra
pick human fruit in a café
choice counters
non consent

Come mares vultures hens women

Let them say we are wonton recipients

guilty of acting while posing as oxygen

Boreas and Zephyrus nymph sluts
immaculate cross pollination

allurement or attunement

Music of the third you

fall in love with love not

a shadow to soothe and regulate call

upon

triage nurse catnip
shift work I confess
incapacity to serve

Rest nervous system shed

plaque heart with

dusk and the queen of wands rise

over the hill

the desire to intervene

like blood on her hands

Once again you
and the point are complete strangers
And not enough of too much has been said

> *All: When the wind blows from the south, that which*
> *no canvas sails could withstand, undress and*
> *conceive by the wind, give birth to girls*

Three Threshing Floors, Three Invisibilities

First

After we hugged in greeting on Christmas, in the visiting room at San Quentin Prison, the first thing Talib said, breaking into a wide smile, was, "Ah, the sound of a baby crying! So wonderful! Among the many kinds of deprivation we live with in here, missing the sounds of the world is a huge one..."

Then we went straight to the vending machines

With our bounty we sat facing each other on the same side of a table.

He told me about his parole appeal. We talked about his memoir and the other writing he does for trade. If someone inside needs their story written he writes it for stamps or other necessities.

Living and writing living — I am Talib's writing "mentor" and
  friend

He had bought photo tokens so we, a Muslim and a Jew, had our picture taken in front of the dusty plastic Christmas tree.

Then it was 1:50 and everyone had to be out by 2pm. We hugged good bye. Thanked each other for the visit. And I joined the crowd of mostly families moving toward the screening exit. A lot of people were crying. I wasn't but I felt emptied, tense, exhausted from being tracked and under scrutiny every second on the way in, while in, and on the way out — and I was only there for a few hours.

On the phone a few weeks later, Talib said, "We've been under the fog line. It means we can't go out on the yard because they might not be able to see us- can't go to the post office either."

You could escape or cross a border in fog, or you could be disappeared in it

Second

In a coal cart on a track I rode
past sleeping lions
underground in an abandoned mine

The wooden cart was no longer used for coal
There was no danger of collapse
The lions were close, but docile as they turned in dreams

of spinning

extraction along the seam

chaff   dross   tailings

into what is happening

what happening is

Of the many guises of that problem: The news, narcissistic parent

delivers inertia, distance, hunger for information

Or "Being held in the mind of the mother [in utero] is the original holding environment... Children not held in the mind of their mother are lost, forgotten."

> (*Neurofeedback in the Treatment of Developmental Trauma*, Sebern Fisher)

If the sight of you is obliterated

you cannot imagine being seen or heard

wordless, or bludgeoned by words

worldless or on my mind

Thus the requirement:

Follow the thread as if there is an outside to the locked room of "etymological despair" (Norma Cole)

The brilliant guy diagnosing why my furnace quit in January

said, "I get better and better at fixing things and I have less and less idea why or how"

Rhythmicity — as Maria and Nicolas Torok call it

Call and response or the answer song as Tyrone Williams calls it

Buzz pollinators striking middle C, or sonication, so I've heard

Third

With their white heads and tails you can spot them from far away.

"Aren't they easy prey?"

Bald eagles are soaring up and down the valley over the river.

"No, because fully grown adults have no known predators.

They are bright so they can see each other," I add, making it up.

"To be born to the world is for each to enter abrupt and knowledgeable into the simple or thrashed truth of one's materiality, knowing that that which is not destined to a relation to the other is worthless."

(*Poetic Intention*, Édouard Glissant, tr. Nathanaël)

The news feeds an emergency dopamine rush that keeps us coming back

("Monetizing Anger," Matt Taibbi)

injects a jagged anti-rhythm, makes us

distracted unsuccessful mourners — melancholics who carry a tomb

who forge from whatever grave informs us — who might hear the answer song without the question

The original holding environment before we can see each other, with the one in the dark inside, mining, listening to one another's turning, breathing, dreaming

The "holding tank," then prison, muffling, secreting from public view, thwarting, thrashing

Like buzz pollinators strike middle C to release pollen, a human voice or tuning fork in middle C will also release pollen

(*Secrets of the Oak Woodlands*, Marianchild)

"The consciousness of the nation is thus consciousness of relation."

(*Poetic Intention*, Glissant)

In a deserted mind

formed when dead plant matter decays into peat converted
into coal by heat and pressure of deep burial over millions of
years lost, forgotten, worthless, gash caesarian land   what
the lions will say on waking, how it burns

Notes for Motion Picture Home

Walter Benjamin, "Theatre and Radio: Toward the Mutual Control of Their Work of Instruction," from *Blaetter des Hessischen Landestheaters*, Darmstadt, 1931/32. Translated by Louis Kaplan. In *Radiotext*(e), Strauss and Mandl, editors, *Semiotext*(e) #16, New York, NY, 1993, 30.

1. Adapted from Clark Blaise, *Time Lord, Sir Sanford Flemming and the Creation of Standard Time*, New York, Pantheon, 2000, xii.

2. Ibid., 23.

3. Paul Rabinow, *Reflections on Fieldwork in Morocco*, Berkeley, University of California Press, 1977, 153.

4. Jessica Benjamin, *Like Subjects, Love Objects*, New Haven and London, Yale UP, 1995, 172 and 174.

5. Blaise, 239.

6. Ibid.

7. Ibid., 227.

 To listen to recorded audio tracks of MPH used in performance

 To watch a video of the play in performance

Kevin Killian directed *Motion Picture Home*, which was written at his request and performed for a Poets Theater Jubilee in San Francisco in 2002. Margaret Tedesco played the Woman. Wayne Smith recorded the sound, and Kota Ezawa coordinated and played the sound during the performance. Tanya Hollis, Taylor Brady, Kevin Killian and Norma Cole performed the offstage Voiceovers, including that of the Teleprompter. In addition to being a live human voice, the Teleprompter character was a huge machine (not a phone-app) lugged onto the stage.

Acknowledgements

Many thanks to the editors of the following journals, chapbook or broadside series where sections of this book first appeared:

—*Hyperborea Or Bermuda Triangles I Have Known*

Chapbook commissioned by Margaret Tedesco on the occasion of the exhibition of Jasmin Lim and Genevieve Quick: I WANT TO STEP ACROSS, on view 12 October to 13 November 2013 at [2nd floor projects], San Francisco.

Hyperborea was also published in *JPR (Journal of Poetic Research)*, John Tranter, editor.

Petroglyph images are from Valcamonica in eastern Lombardy, Italy, circa 1,000 BCE.

—G I V E

Thanks to Headlands Center for the Arts, Sausalito, California, for the residency that propelled, supported, provided the time, a studio and much of the geography of this work.

An early version of *G I V E* appeared in *Second Stutter,* Colin Partch and Solomon Rino, editors.

Brenda Iijima, publisher of YoYo Labs, made a beautiful broadside of a section of *G I V E*.

—The Wind in Her Daughtership's Majesty

Thanks to Evan Kennedy whose great book *Terra Firmament* was among the sparks for *The Wind….* Parts of the poem are translations of *Terra Firmament*.

Sections were published in *The Chicago Review #MeToo: A Poetry Collective*, Emily Critchley and Elizabeth-Jane Burnett, editors.

Excerpts in *spoKe*, Sunnylyn Thibodeaux, guest editor.

Excerpts in guest editor Laynie Browne's *Solidarity Texts* section of *Jacket2*.

Excerpts in *Elderly*, Jamie Townsend and Nick DeBoer, editors.

—*Three Threshing Floors, Three Invisibilities*

Many thanks to my friend and student Charles Talib Brooks, for friendship and permission to include this piece in this book.

The poem first appeared in *The Brooklyn Rail*, Norma Cole, guest poetry critic, in response to her "From the Threshing Floor."

Deepest gratitude to Ghazal Mosadeq and Hamed Jaberha of Pamenar Press for their support of this book, from enthusiasm to design to conversation. Your work and attention is sustenance.

Big thanks also to Eleni Stecopoulos and Steve Dickison for their acute eyes, ears and thoughts. Their time and attention have sharpened this work in ways otherwise not possible. Thank you to Norma Cole, Laura Moriarty, Steve Seidenberg, Susan Thackrey, Justin Robinson, Margaret Tedesco, Eleni Stecopoulos, Steve Dickison, Phoebe Giannisi, Will Alexander, Helen Dimos , Stephen Motika, George Albon, Julia Dresher,

CJ Martin, Evan Kennedy, Kevin Killian, and many others, alive and not, for your accompaniment in friendship and poetry. You make it possible.

Lightning Source UK Ltd.
Milton Keynes UK
UKHW041043131022
410414UK00005B/110